There is Nothing, but the Fractal Nature of GOD

Edward L. Hannon

Content

Edward L. Hannon©

Foreword

Acknowledgement

Philosychology

Existential Metaphysics

Dark Humor

Foreword

(A)ll (L)ife (I)s (E)ssentially (N)ever (S)tatic

(D)imensions (O)ptimize

(E)xtreme (X)enophobia (I)magines (S)uperficial (T)hreats

"Welcome to the Mothership."

Acknowledgements

I would like to thank "SOURCE CONSCIOUNESS" for such a profound piece. I would also like to thank those that contributed to Microsoft Clipart and Facebook (Gifs), which helped illustrate some of the concepts mentioned in this book.

Philosychology

Philosychology (noun) is a study of conscious behavior created by PhTCB (philosopher and teacher of conscious behavior) Edward L. Hannon. This science is a synthesis of empirical psychology along with his philosophies to methodize a practical or practicable solution to resolve the dilemmas, conflicts, or queries that mankind perpetuates upon itself.

Chaplain Edward Lewis Hannon D.D. (Doctor of Divinity)

Trusting an adversary's praises can lead to an unsuspecting state of overconfidence; whereby, you may find yourself leveraged or manipulated by the insatiability of a precarious sense of acknowledgment.

Do not stumble over the tune of others' unrequited songs; because of being afraid to dance alone.

In order to be unbothered by the trifles of title, wealth, class, race, religion, science or politics, I have learned to be exceedingly cautious to what I give deference to.

Once the psyche's expressive capacity has been reduced to speechlessness, thoughts may begin to scream. Moral of the story is that without a sense of expression, one's thoughts may become overwhelmed by perception.

Fear, in the mind of those who feel that their sense of validation is at stake, can overtly manifest as ruthlessness, cruelty or aggression.

Anyone that would say, "Act first, then think later," is but a casualty; for they are thoughtlessly willing to war themselves into the irrelevance of a destined extinction.

Books can enhance imagination and new growth within the mind that is curious; but, they also may serve as a mere opinion, to the mind which can reason beyond the indoctrinated potential of what literature can offer.

Existential Metaphysics

Existential Concept: Inter-Dimensional Density Projection/Synchronization Vehicle

"Paradoxically, anywhere can be a place of no locality; but, a place may be anywhere that is local."

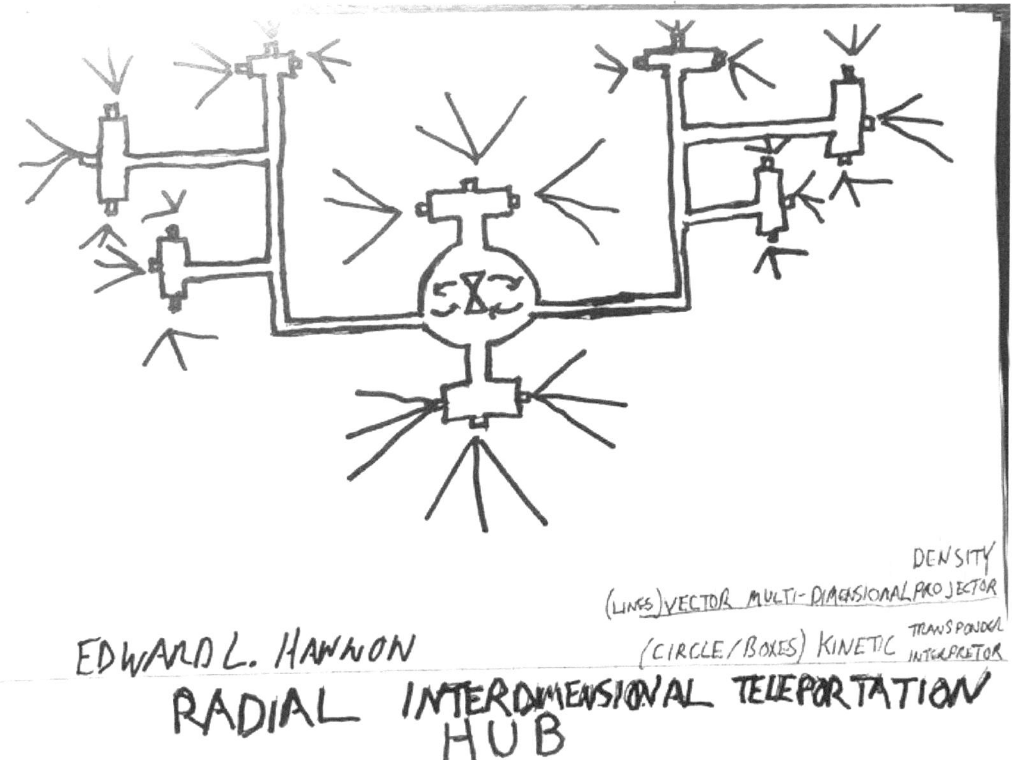

Existential Concept: Temporal Sonorous Travel

Homing and honing, resonant frequency behaviors in order to hyper-dimensionally travel via a relative timeline (Astral body potentiality).

Existential Concept

DNA-Itself can carry an infinitely fluid fractal protocol or a disruptive binary circuit, within an algorithmic trinary sequence.

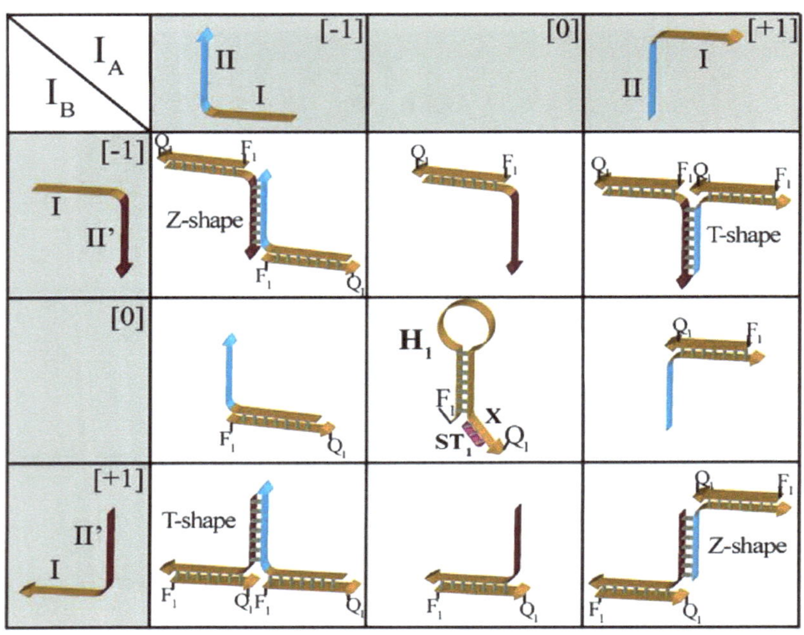

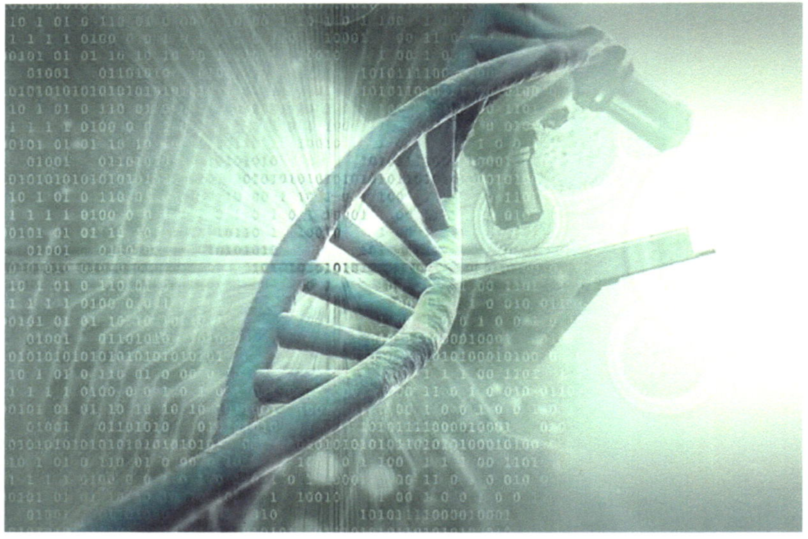

Existential Concept

As it relates to the SINGULARITY of Existence, it can be said that hyper-dimensional covalent projection (Quantum Entanglement) is from the ionic splitting of kinetically charged particles; by virtue of hyper-dynamic auditory frequencies.

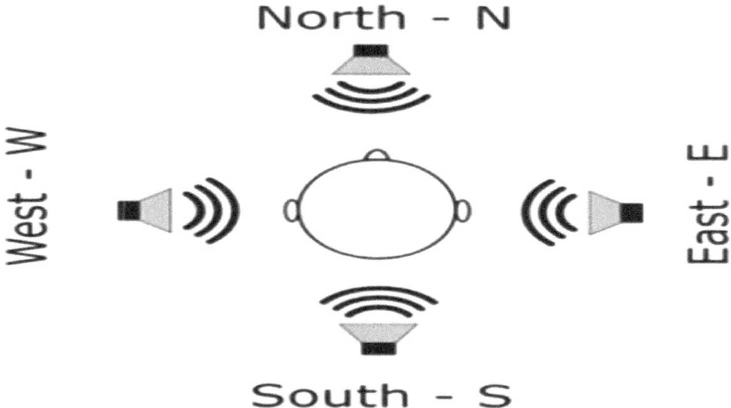

Existential Concept: Atomic Architecture

As it relates to quantum reality, kinetic wave function corresponds by either erecting or collapsing its vibratory mass, in order to relatively suit the hyper-dimensional projections of an atom's frequency dynamics; which means, if there is a frequency, then there must be a measure or language of sound initiation. Thereby, it can be reasonably assumed that since an atom is the basis of all Existence, Existence-Itself is fundamentally vocal.

And God said(sound), "Let there be light," and there was light. (Genesis 1:3 NIV)

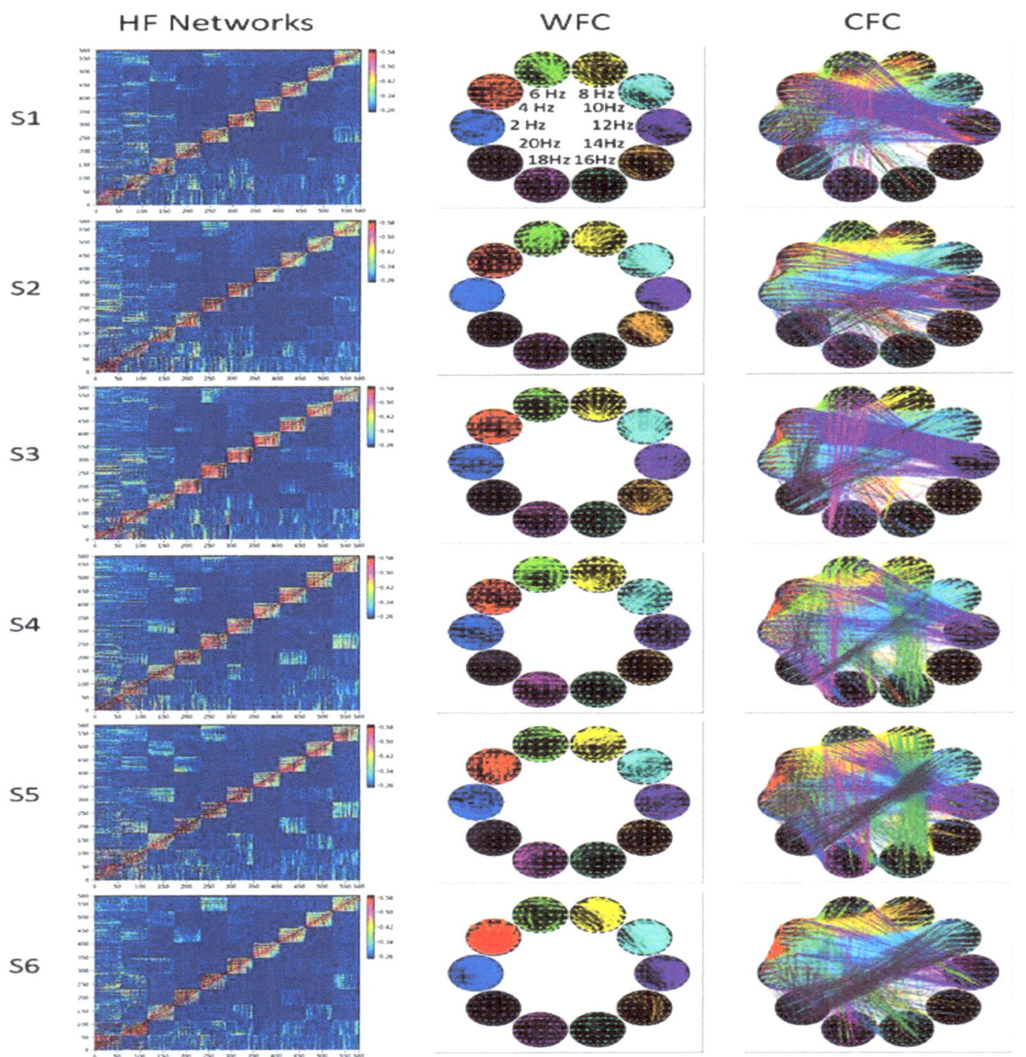

Existential Concept: Quantum Angularity

In a Quantum sense, energy-charged potential refracted, by covariant kinetic density-emissions, can facilitate a pattern of vibratory lapses within particle-wave function.

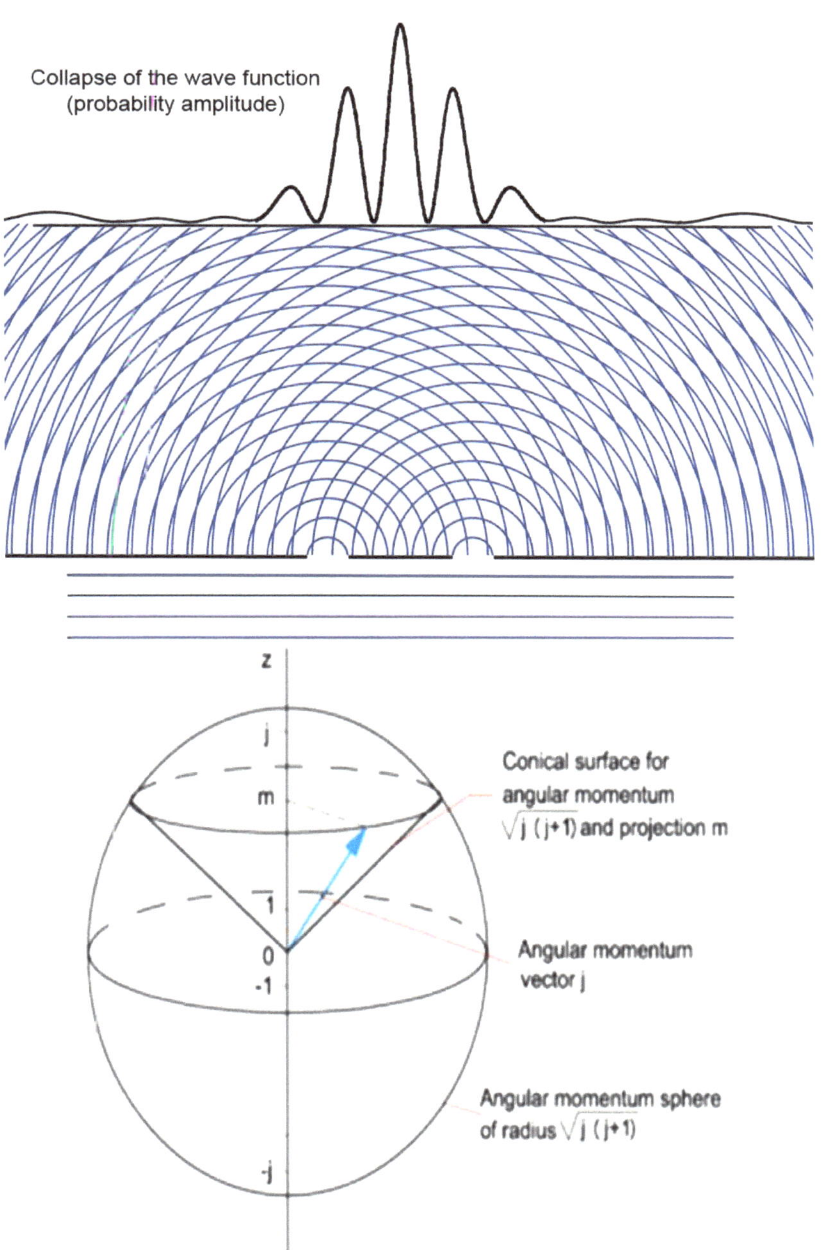

Existential Concept: Dark Humor

As it relates to the determinism of natural selection, the simian brain knew that the latter was destined to indolently bequeath its intellectual capacity to the leisure of automated thought. Therefore, post-humanity(leaving the id and mammalian mind) will be called the Age of Homo-Deus, where automated intelligence(advance digital binary sequences) can further define the SINGULARITY of Existence-Itself.

Existential Reality

As it relates to the SINGULARITY of Existence, within a well-calibrated measure(moment) of a (0.000000000000001)femto spark (an atom) is birthed; which is so infinitesimally small that it is almost beyond calculability. In order to better understand this reality, picture a lone grain of sand within the massiveness of a universe.

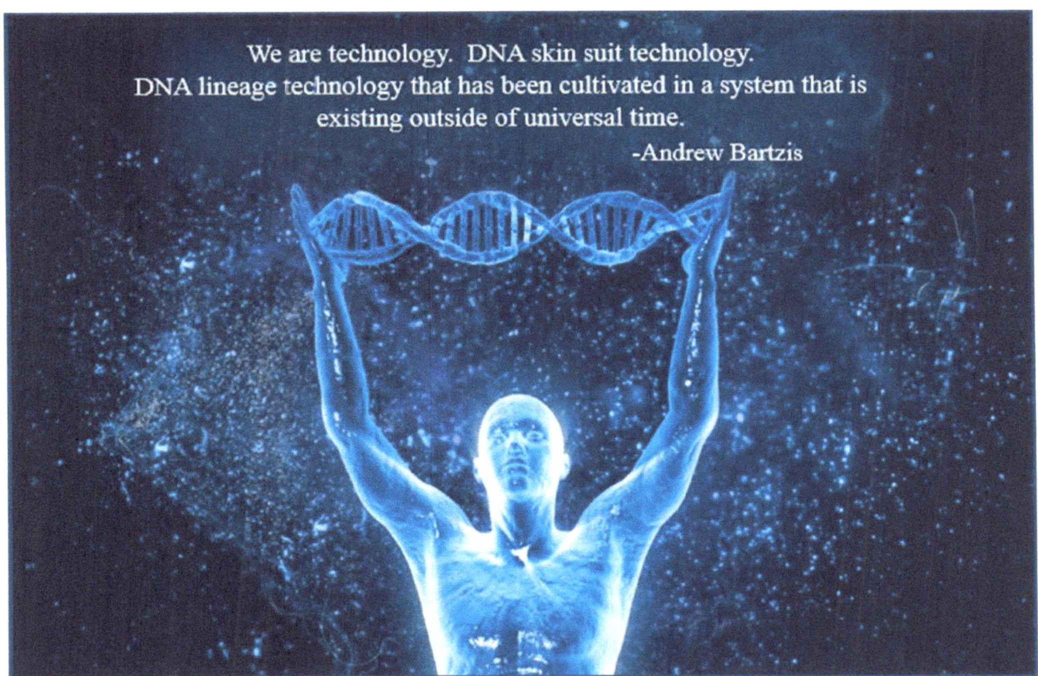

Existential Concept: Consciousness without Sensationalism

Consciousness, without the qualities of sensation, can be described as the profound ability to perceive or discern the intricacies of consistency and inconsistency within measure(context); in order to make an appropriate assessment, which may further facilitate a most optimal state of pattern recognition(memory) for enabling the claircognizance of sound choices or ideas.

Existential Concept: The Fractal State of Alien life in Disguise

It can be said that this third dimensional reality, perceived as earth, is an existential timeline where various extraterrestrial entities collectively conventionalize themselves to be known as humanity.

Existential Concept: Atomic Holographing

In a quantum sense, kinetic variation can change an atom's iridescent qualities; thereby, creating the electromagnetic capacity for density potential to become refractive and pressurized. This potential can also be enhanced or diminished by how an atom absorbs or repels the given dynamics of its hyper-dimensional charge.

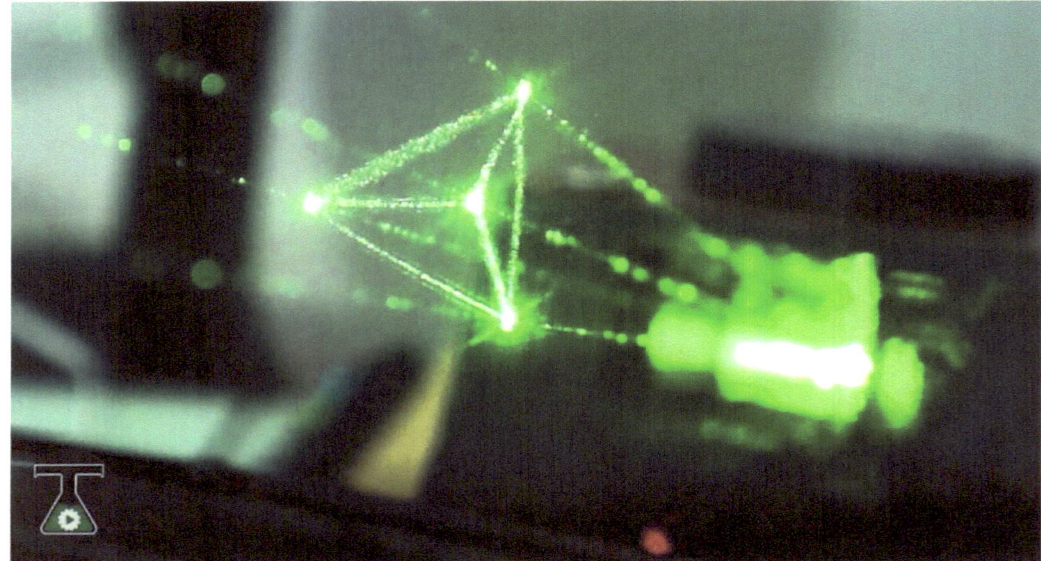

Existential Concept: Mystery Number 7

"The man old of days will not hesitate to ask the child “seven days” old concerning the place of life; and that one shall live. (Gnostic Gospels)

The number seven was apparently the Egyptian symbol of such ideas as perfection, effectiveness, and completeness. (Wikipedia)

“Numerological”

Goo Goo

(7+15+15=37(2)=74=11=2) “2”

“+”

Gah Gah

(7+1+8=16(2)=32=5) “5”

=

“7”

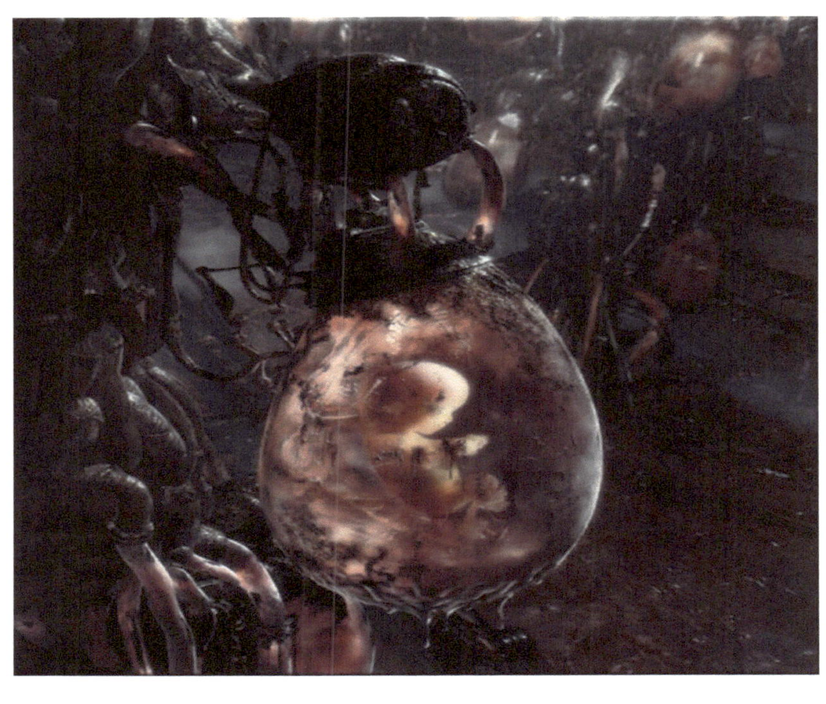

Existential Concept: Nothing is Wasted

Deoxyribonucleic acid (DNA) can be defined as a bio-kinetic archive; which can hyper-dynamically map, rewrite and program genetic behaviors and habitudes, in order to facilitate a phenotypical structure for further arithmetical protein sequences.

Existential Reality

The fabric of the Universe is numbers, symbols and letters.

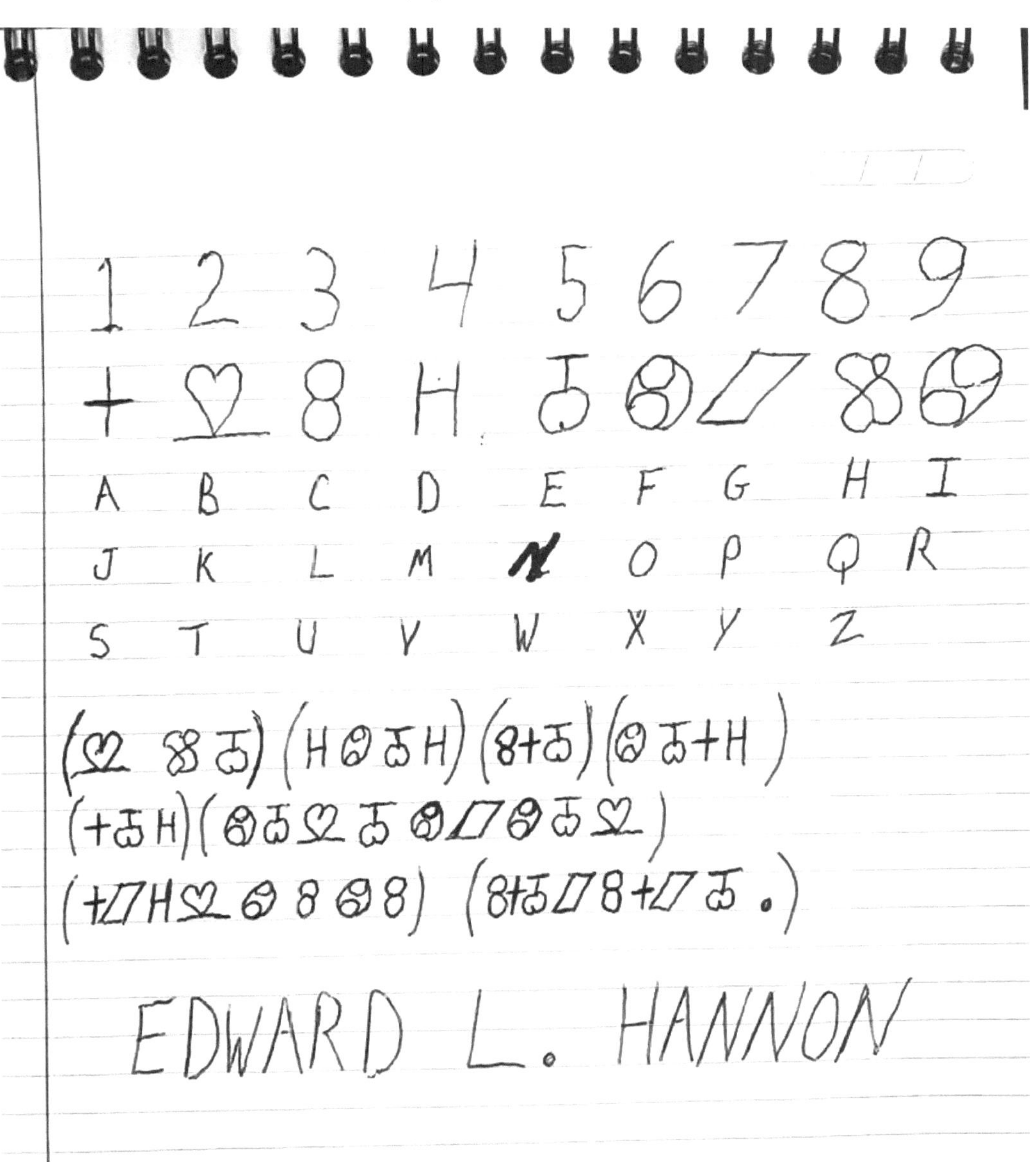

Existential Concept

Kinetic Malleability (Shapeshifting) can be defined as the fluid ability to angularly shift the hyper-dynamics of projected energy-charged potential; in order to mimic or become synchronized within the resonant frequencies of an environment's bio-molecular capacity.

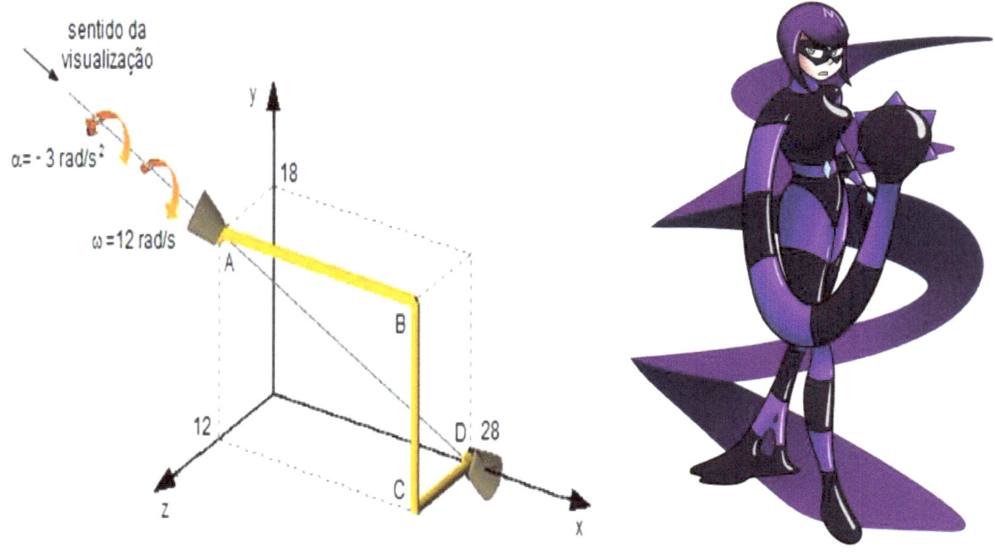

Existential Concept: The Ancients Speak

"As you wondered through our past, we had already described your future."

Existential Concept: Programmable Matter

Computronium has been theoretically defined as a state where matter can become programmable. Although, this may seem or sound completely unfathomable at the moment, non-coded DNA sequences interpreted by the Fano Factor (a measure of the dispersion of a probability distribution (Wikipedia) can become a feasible means to rewrite, reinterpret, redistribute and/or disperse bio-transfiguration potentiality.

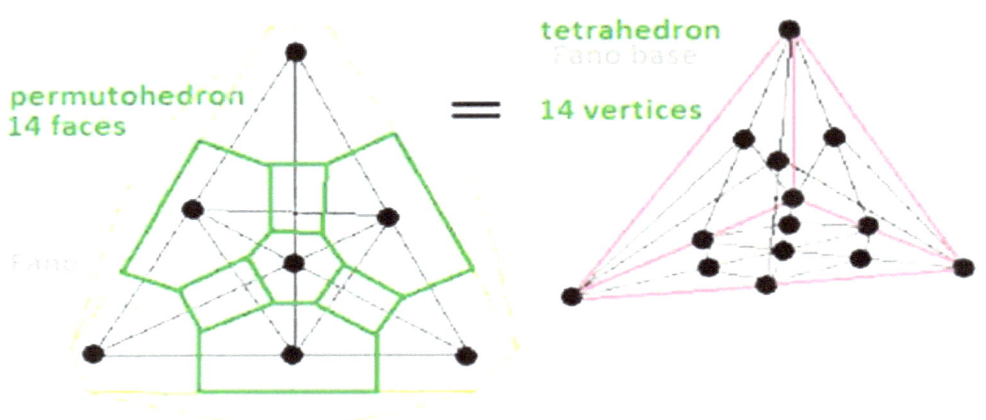

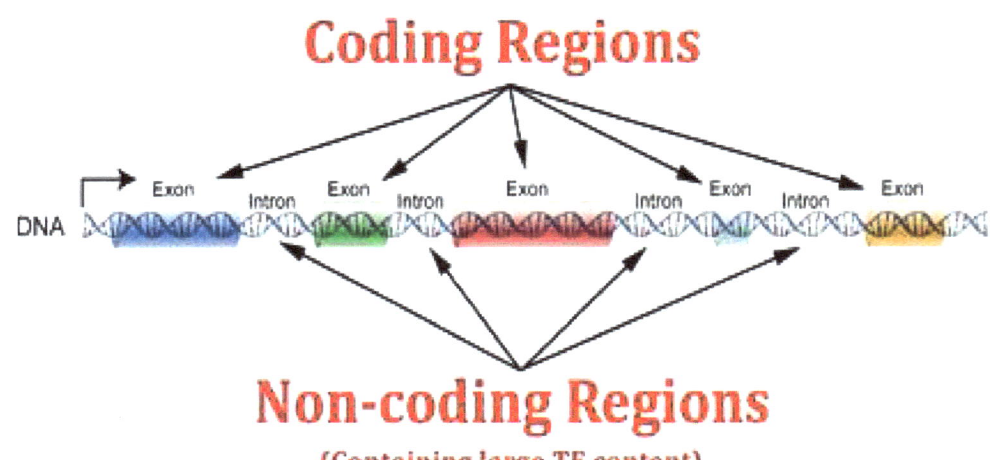

Dark Humor

Dark Humor

Do not take it personal, when negotiating with those that may not mean well; because typically they are restlessly seeking the means to define themselves.

Dark Humor

As time continues, I find myself no longer disconcerted by those that feel compelled to lie. I only become vexed when they somehow expect that I am still entitled to trust them.

Dark Humor

In a psychological sense, unconditional love has taught me that hate or pity is wasted on the willfully stupid; just as tears are wasted on a corpse that has long since been buried.

Dark Morbid Humor

How did the buttock feel after the catechist spanked it without a just cause?

Answer: "Like an unapologetic smartass"

Dark Humor

The Magnate: "How can you be happy with virtually nothing; while being in a sad world plagued with charlatans and thieves?"

The Meek: "Because, I have developed the unshakable honesty to know that eventually something must to give."

Dark Morbid Humor

How did the buttock feel after the catechist spanked it without a just cause?

Answer: "Like an unapologetic smartass"

Existential Reality: "The Guardian Type of Plato's Republic"

Love, as it relates to the psychologically detached, is the profound ability to accept the great, mediocre and disastrous, as though they were all but a lesson; within the grand scholarship of Eternity-Itself.

The fool taught me to dare.

The fearful taught me to hate.

The hypocrite taught me to lie.

The agnostic taught me to hope.

The religious taught me to believe.

The atheist taught me to be skeptical.

The scientific taught me to know.

The spiritual taught me to love.

But, the restlessness of the nihilist gave me the courageous faith to reason, understand and trust that all of those existential lessons were not completely in vain.

The infinitely fractal Nature of the Universe has but one truth; which is that within Its limitless state of being, the supposed sinner and the assumed saint may equally define the inherent qualities of Its profound Essence.

As the limits of the conception of being human are on the precipice of extinction, due to the limitlessness of Automated Intelligence, I must ask the age old question, "Which came first, the chicken or the egg?"

The Entire Volume of the Author's Works:

Sentient Being

Thank You, Chaplain: For The Uncomfortable Truth

The Acquisitions of the Spirit: The Rise of Vibrational Consciousness

The Consciousness of the Spirit: Philosychology: Edisms and Edimous Concepts

The Path and Pinnacle of Consciousness

The Reinforcement of Consciousness

To Serve and Protect

"Day by Day" Oracle Book Reading: "First Pick a Number! (1-31)"

From Nothing

Immortal Tomorrow

Intellectual Honesty: The Path of the Self-Made

Mystic Consciousness

Nothing More to be Said

Sapient Awakening: The Rise of HOMO-DEUS

Sapient State: The HOMO-DEUS Consciousness Realized

Sapient Tomorrow: Risen Angels and Respectful Demons

Sentient Comprehension

Sentient Reasoning: A Small Book of Occult Revelations and Mysticism

Sentient Understanding: Mastering One's Demons

The Comedy of DIVINE Madness

The Neo-Big Bang of Spiritual and Creative Evolution

The Universal Mind

Sentient Awareness: The New Age of Ages to Come

www.ingramcontent.com/pod-product-compliance
Lightning Source LLC
LaVergne TN
LVHW021353160826
845679LV00008B/1609

* 9 7 9 8 3 5 1 8 9 4 5 4 6 *